spot

OCEAN ANIMALS

SHARKS

by Mari Schuh

AMICUS | AMICUS INK

fin

gills

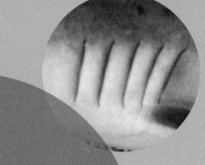

Look for these words and pictures as you read.

snout

teeth

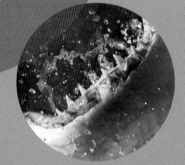

A shark swims in circles.
Look at it go!

Sharks live in every ocean.
They are fish.

Look at the fin.
It keeps sharks from rolling over.
It helps them turn.

fin

Look at the gills. They are slits.
Gills help sharks breathe underwater.

gills

Look at its snout.

It smells for fish to eat.

It smells for seals, too.

snout

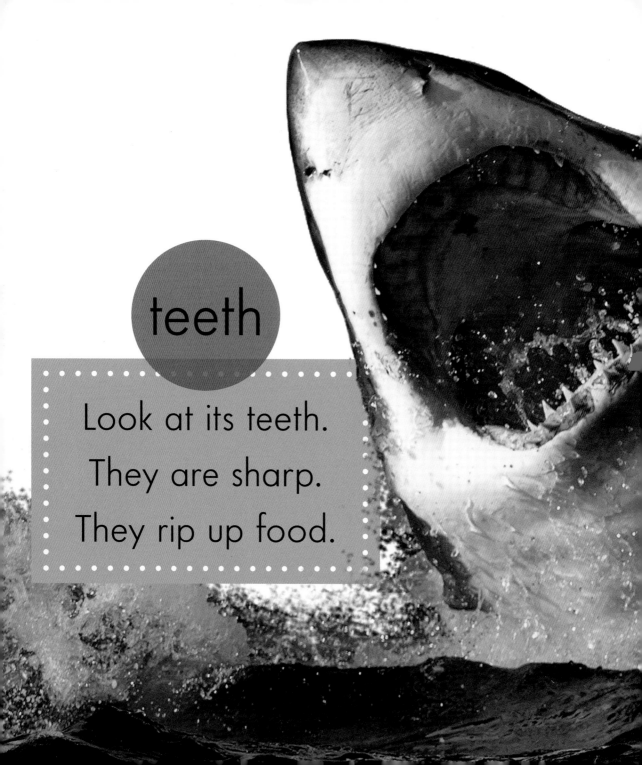

teeth

Look at its teeth.
They are sharp.
They rip up food.

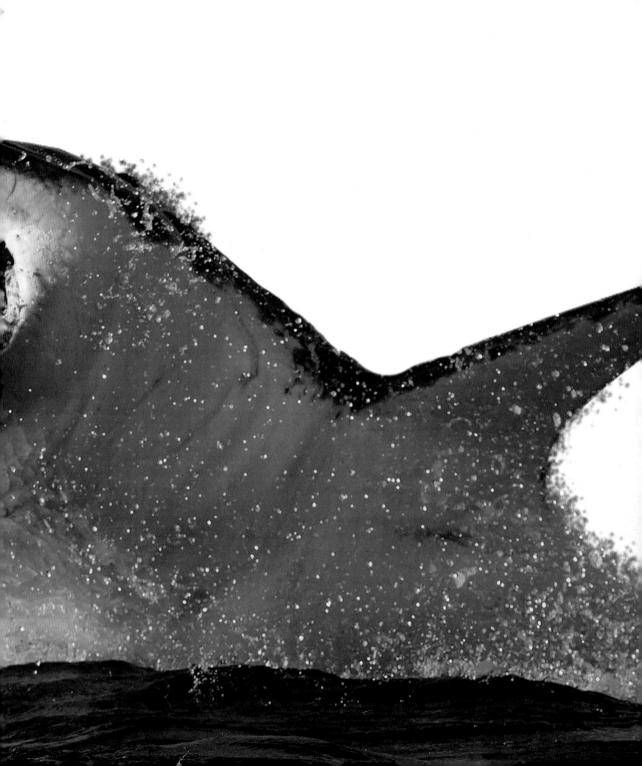

Look at the ocean floor.
A shark hunts.
What will it find?

fin

Look at the fin.
It keeps sharks from rolling over.
It helps them turn.
fin

gills

Look at the gills. They are slits.
Gills help sharks breathe underwater.
gills

Did you find?

snout

Look at its snout.
It smells for fish to eat.
It smells for seals, too.
snout

teeth

teeth
Look at its teeth.
They are sharp.
They rip up food.

spot

Spot is published by Amicus and Amicus Ink
P.O. Box 1329, Mankato, MN 56002
www.amicuspublishing.us

Library of Congress Cataloging-in-Publication Data
Names: Schuh, Mari C., 1975- author.
Title: Sharks / by Mari Schuh.
Description: Mankato, Minnesota : Spot/Amicus, [2019] |
   Series: Ocean animals | Audience: K to grade 3.
Identifiers: LCCN 2017020474| ISBN 9781681513836
   (library binding) | ISBN 9781681514659 (ebook) | ISBN
   9781681523033 (paperback)
Subjects: LCSH: Sharks--Juvenile literature.
Classification: LCC QL638.9 .S2928 2019 |
   DDC 597.3--dc23
LC record available at https://lccn.loc.gov/2017020474

Printed in China

HC   10 9 8 7 6 5 4 3 2 1
PB   10 9 8 7 6 5 4 3 2 1

For Natalie, a young shark lover –MS

Rebecca Glaser, editor
Deb Miner, series designer
Ciara Beitlich, book designer
Holly Young, photo researcher

Photos by Getty Images/Jim Abernethy,
4–5; 5-Apr; iStockPhoto/atese, 8–9;
USO, 12–13; Shutterstock/Ramon
Carretero, cover, 16, Matt9122, 1,
solarseven, 3, LeonP, 6–7, art nick,
10–11, Damsea, 14–15

SHARKS